ELIZABETH BLACKWELL

America's First Female Doctor

"It is not easy to be a pioneer—but oh, it is fascinating! I would not trade one moment, even the worst moment, for all the riches in the world." — Elizabeth Blackwell

Life Portraits

ELIZABETH BLACKWELL
America's First Female Doctor

By Barbara A. Somervill

Gareth Stevens
Publishing

Please visit our web site at **www.garethstevens.com.**
For a free catalog describing Gareth Stevens Publishing's list of high-quality books,
call 1-800-542-2595 (USA) or 1-800-387-3178 (Canada).
Gareth Stevens Publishing's fax: 1-877-542-2596

Library of Congress Cataloging-in-Publication Data
Somervill, Barbara A.
   Elizabeth Blackwell: America's first female doctor / by Barbara A. Somervill.
     p. cm. — (Life portraits)
   Includes bibliographical references and index.
   ISBN-10: 1-4339-0055-6   ISBN-13: 978-1-4339-0055-6 (lib. bdg.)
    1. Blackwell, Elizabeth, 1821-1910. 2. Women physicians—United States—
Biography. 3. Physicians—United States—Biography. I. Title.
R154.B623S66   2009
610.82092—dc22
  [B]   2008036607

This edition first published in 2009 by
Gareth Stevens Publishing
A Weekly Reader® Company
1 Reader's Digest Rd.
Pleasantville, NY 10570-7000 USA

Copyright © 2009 by Gareth Stevens, Inc.

Executive Managing Editor: Lisa M. Herrington
Creative Director: Lisa Donovan
Cover Designer: Keith Plechaty
Interior Designers: Yin Ling Wong and Keith Plechaty
Publisher: Keith Garton

Produced by Spooky Cheetah Press
www.spookycheetah.com
Editor: Stephanie Fitzgerald
Designer: Kimberly Shake
Cartographer: XNR Productions, Inc.
Proofreader: Jessica Cohn
Indexer: Madge Walls, All Sky Indexing

Printed in the United States of America

1 2 3 4 5 6 7 8 9 12 11 10 09 08

TABLE OF CONTENTS

Elizabeth Blackwell challenged the medical world—and society's ideas about women—to become America's first female physician.

CHAPTER ONE

A Woman Doctor! What Next?

Frost hung in the air on a bright, sunny winter day in Geneva, New York. It was January 23, 1849—graduation day for the Geneva Medical College. At 10 A.M., a group of male students gathered together on the college grounds. Together they paraded to Presbyterian House, the church where the graduation ceremony would take place. There was music and joking, and the men were full of high spirits. They had worked hard to earn their degrees, and the budding young physicians were ready to celebrate. The Bishop of New York, Dr. Hale (the president of the school), and faculty members led the enthusiastic students toward the hall. Interestingly, the only person missing from the group was the one everyone wanted to see—Elizabeth Blackwell.

Dr. James Webster, Elizabeth's favorite professor, had asked more than once if Elizabeth would join in the parade. She refused.

According to Elizabeth, "It wouldn't be ladylike." She wanted to make a good impression on the people attending the graduation. She had come far in life, but Elizabeth still had plenty to prove to the people of Geneva and the medical community at large. She worried that some people might think she was silly or irresponsible if she joked along with the lighthearted men.

Instead, Elizabeth and her brother Henry made their way quietly to the Presbyterian House for the ceremony. They sat in the back of the church, waiting for Elizabeth's fellow graduates to arrive. When the other students entered the building, Elizabeth would join them. She seemed calm and in control as she sat next to her brother. If she really was calm, Elizabeth may have been the only person in the church who was. Excitement practically buzzed in the air.

Women from Geneva packed the church. When Elizabeth first arrived in town, she met with a lot of disapproval. People didn't like the idea of allowing a woman to attend medical school. Now they turned out in large numbers to see the graduation of "the female student." Margaret Munro DeLancey, a young woman who attended the ceremony, recalled:

> *Annie and I went down early to the 'Presbyterian House' but though there a full hour before the exercises commenced yet we were unable to get a front seat in the gallery … About half past ten … the procession entered the building. The Lioness of the day, Miss Blackwell met them at the door and entered with the Medical Students, without hat or shawl.*

A HISTORIC MOMENT

There were 17 students in Elizabeth's class. The male students went up in groups of four to receive their diplomas. Finally, after the last man received his certificate, Elizabeth was called to the stage. She went up alone. As Elizabeth approached Dr. Hale, he rose, took off his hat, and bowed. Accepting the diploma, Elizabeth said,

Elizabeth was very proud to receive her diploma from Geneva Medical College in 1849.

"Sir, I thank you; by the help of the Most High, it shall be the effort of my life to shed honor upon your diploma." The two bowed to each other, and then Elizabeth rejoined her fellow graduating doctors.

Dr. Charles Lee, dean of Geneva Medical College, then delivered the valedictory address to the crowd. In his speech, he praised Elizabeth for her devotion and hard work in studying medicine. He said that she "was fully qualified to practice as a Physician, and that the degree was fully merited." It was the answer to the question that was on the minds of many. Dr. Lee ended his speech saying, "God speed her … in her errand of mercy, and crown her efforts with … success!" At that, loud applause filled the church. The first woman medical doctor in the United States had received her diploma. Not only that—she had finished first in her class!

Elizabeth's graduation ceremony took place in the Presbyterian House church on the Geneva College campus.

PUBLIC REACTION

The commencement ceremony was much like other college graduations at the time. This particular graduation made a lasting impact on medicine in the United States and Europe, however. Elizabeth Blackwell was a pioneer, a leader—and now a doctor.

The event drew attention around the world. Some people believed women were not suited to become doctors. They thought women should be wives, mothers, and homemakers. They did not think women were smart enough to be doctors or strong enough to handle the work. Even Dr. Lee, who praised Elizabeth at her graduation, did not think women should be doctors. He believed she might be an excellent physician but hoped no other women would follow her lead. Dr. Lee accepted Elizabeth as unique. He did not expect to ever see another woman as gifted, dedicated, or intelligent as she was entering the medical field.

> "Woman was obviously designed to move in another sphere, to discharge other duties ... The course of 'domina Blackwell' cannot be justified."
>
> – D.K.

A letter of protest appeared in the *Boston Medical and Surgical Journal*. Written by "D.K.," the letter stated that "Woman was obviously designed to move in another sphere, to discharge other duties—not less important, not less honorable ... but more refined, more delicate. ... The course of 'domina Blackwell' cannot be justified."

Not all public reactions were negative. *Punch,* a humorous magazine in Great Britain, ran a poem in Elizabeth's honor:

Young ladies all, of every clime
Especially of Britain
Who wholly occupy your time
In novels or in knittin'
Whose highest skill is but to play
Sing, dance, or French to clack well,
Reflect on the example, pray
Of excellent Miss Blackwell!

Education for Women in the 1800s

It was hard for women to get an education in the 1800s. Boston and New York did not even allow girls to go to high school until 1826. In 1829, social reformer Fanny Wright gave public speeches about equal education for women. Most people thought she was crazy. Society believed that women were not physically or mentally capable of learning the same subjects or doing the same jobs as men. Some thought that an educated woman would be an unfit mother. Mount Holyoke, the first women's college, was founded in 1837 in Massachusetts.

Coeducational colleges were slow to develop, too. The first to accept both men and women was Oberlin College in Ohio in 1833. Most of the colleges that taught both men and women in the late 1800s were in the Midwest. Slowly college education became more available to women. However, it wasn't until 1980 that the number of women college students in the United States equaled the number of male students.

Public opinion mattered little, however. It was too late to stop Elizabeth Blackwell. She had her degree. She was America's first woman doctor. The door was now open, and many more women would follow Elizabeth's lead. Women who wanted to become doctors looked to her as a beacon of hope. Within just three years, 20 other women had graduated from American medical schools. Gaining a degree was just a first step, though. Getting hospitals and patients to accept women as doctors would take serious effort. Elizabeth had won the first battle, but she still had the rest of the war to fight. ❖

Samuel and Hannah Blackwell could never have imagined that their third child, Elizabeth, would make such an impact on the world of medicine.

CHAPTER TWO

FAMILY TIES, FAMILY STRUGGLES

IN 1815, SAMUEL BLACKWELL MET AND MARRIED Hannah Lane, a pious, Congregationalist Sunday school teacher. They married on September 27, 1815, in Bristol, England, and started their family right away. A year after they married, the Blackwell's first child, Anna, arrived. Two years later, Marian was born. A son, Samuel Charles, who died as an infant, followed Marian. Elizabeth, the third daughter, was born on February 3, 1821. After Elizabeth, the Blackwells had another son, also named Samuel Charles, but that child died, too.

When Elizabeth was 2 years old, yet another, healthy Samuel Charles was born. Henry followed in 1825, and Emily arrived a year later. Ellen was born in 1828, and Howard followed in 1831. In addition to the family's many children, four unmarried aunts lived with the Blackwells. The two Blackwell parents, four aunts, and eight children made for a lively household.

AN UNUSUAL UPBRINGING

The Blackwells belonged to the Bridge Street Congregational Church. The family followed the church's teachings for the most part. They followed their own thoughts about things they believed should be outside church control, however. Sometimes church teachings and family beliefs conflicted.

The family's church openly opposed slavery. Samuel owned a sugar refinery, and sugar was the product of slave labor in the Caribbean. The sugar refinery processed raw sugar into two different products: molasses and refined sugar. Molasses was used to make rum. Refined sugar was used to make sweetened food. Samuel was torn. He despised the idea of slavery and supported

This sugar refinery is much like the one owned by Elizabeth's father in the early 1800s. The sugar trade relied heavily on slave labor—a fact that caused Samuel Blackwell much distress.

ending the practice of owning slaves. In his free time, he worked as an abolitionist to end slavery. Yet he needed to make money. He had a large, growing family to support, and the sugar trade paid well.

Church members read the Bible but were not supposed to read novels. Dancing and music were frowned upon. The Blackwells danced, played music, and read novels. Unlike many parents of the time, Samuel and Hannah treated their children equally. They believed it was important for both girls and boys to be educated. They hired tutors to teach their children and encouraged the kids to study hard. In the 1800s, the idea of a family sending all the children to school was a new one in England. Most people who could afford to hire a teacher or governess had their children educated at home. For many girls, education meant French, music, painting, and sewing. The Blackwell girls were lucky to learn science, math, and literature.

FAMILY FORTUNES

In 1828, the Blackwell sugar refinery burned down. Later in life, Anna recalled the event:

> *I can see the whole household, children, servants, Mama, Aunts, all huddled against the railings at the top of Bridge St. ... watching the great feathers of flame, and the volumes of sparks, rushing up into the sky.*

The fire cost Samuel most of his fortune. The family struggled to make ends meet. Unfortunately, the fire was not the only financial loss for the Blackwells. Samuel also lost money on investments in Ireland. Trying to keep expenses low, Samuel bought a new sugar refinery with a house next door. The family moved to their new home in 1828.

Shortly after the Blackwells moved, political riots caused trouble in Bristol. What began as parades, speeches, and protests ended in violence. Samuel was afraid to let the children go out. The Blackwells worried about the growing dangers of being in the city and wondered if they truly had a future in England.

By the time Elizabeth turned 11, her father was deep in debt. Samuel and Hannah decided to leave Bristol and England. The Blackwells, like many other Europeans during that time, went to America in search of a better life.

JOURNEY TO THE NEW WORLD

In August 1832, Elizabeth and her family left for New York aboard the *Cosmo*. Their party included Samuel, Hannah (who was pregnant again), their eight children, a governess, two servants, and two of the aunts. Although they traveled in cabins, the ship's rooms were crowded, and the trip was a nightmare. The family ate salt beef or pork and hard biscuits. They drank foul-tasting water and ate spoonfuls of arrowroot jelly to stop seasickness. Elizabeth suffered miserably from seasickness, which was a problem that bothered her all her life. The trip took nearly two months. The Blackwells were more than delighted when the *Cosmo* finally dropped anchor in New York Harbor.

When the Blackwells arrived in New York, they found a house on Thompson Street, just off Washington Square. The house was not quite as elegant as their home in Bristol, but it would have to

For hundreds of years, immigrants have poured into the United States looking for a better life. When the Blackwells entered New York Harbor in 1832, there was no Statue of Liberty to greet them. The famous monument was dedicated in 1886.

do. The children immediately entered school. The family found a Congregational church nearby. They quickly became involved in church activities, including the anti-slavery cause. A few weeks after the Blackwells arrived, Hannah welcomed her ninth child, a son named George Washington Blackwell.

In 1835, Samuel and Hannah decided to move to Flushing, across the East River on Long Island. Housing was cheaper, and the Blackwells would have more room. Unfortunately, the move was a disaster. Flushing was little more than a mosquito-infested swamp. Samuel Blackwell caught malaria, which is passed on by the bite of infected mosquitoes. People with malaria suffer from fevers and chills, headaches, and weakness.

The Blackwells did not stay in New York very long. After moving to New Jersey, Elizabeth and her siblings traveled to New York to attend school, though.

The next move took the family across the Hudson River to New Jersey in 1836. Jersey City was a small suburb with cheap housing. This was a necessity: Elizabeth's father was not making enough money to support the family.

The older children continued to attend their New York City school, traveling back and forth by ferry every day with their father. Elizabeth later described her new lifestyle:

> *As daily pupils in an excellent school in New York,*
> *entering ardently into the anti-slavery struggle, attending*
> *meetings and societies, the years passed rapidly away …*
> *We became acquainted with William Lloyd Garrison and*

other noble leaders in the long and arduous anti-slavery struggle. Garrison was a welcome guest in our home. He was very fond of children, and would delight them with long repetitions of Russian poetry.

William Lloyd Garrison

William Lloyd Garrison (1805–1879) was born in Newburyport, Massachusetts. His family was poor. As a child, he sold candy, delivered wood, and apprenticed at a newspaper. As an adult, Garrison worked as a newspaper writer and editor. He fought slavery through the Anti-Slavery Society and through his newspaper, the *Liberator*. When Garrison published his first issue of the *Liberator* in 1831, he said, "I do not wish to think, or speak, or write with moderation. ... I am in earnest—I will not equivocate—I will not excuse—I will not retreat a single inch—AND I WILL BE HEARD." For more than 30 years, Garrison fought passionately for the rights of African Americans.

He became a friend of the Blackwells when the family worked against slavery in New York City.

The abolitionists disapproved of the sugar industry, but this did not stop them from becoming close friends with the Blackwells. The family attended abolitionist fairs at which famous speakers criticized the practice of owning slaves. Yet, all the while, the Blackwells lived off money earned from slavery.

In 1836, the Gower, Guppy and Co. refinery where Samuel worked caught fire and suffered serious damage. Gower, one of the owners, had no interest in rebuilding. Samuel also owned a refinery at the time. Shortly after the Gower, Guppy fire, Samuel sold his refinery and began planning a move west.

Once again the Blackwells found themselves in a disastrous financial situation. This time, however, the crisis was national, not personal. In 1837, jobs were scarce, and most paper money

The Anti-Slavery Movement in New York

New York City served as the headquarters for the American Anti-Slavery Society from 1833 to 1870. William Lloyd Garrison and Arthur Tappan founded the group. African American Frederick Douglass and freed slave William Brown were popular speakers for the society. By 1838, the American Anti-Slavery Society had more than 1,300 chapters and 250,000 members. The group held fairs to teach visitors about the evils of slavery and earn money to support their causes. The Blackwells participated in these fairs, selling sugar kisses—a type of candy—and flags.

was worthless. Prices skyrocketed. Few people could buy food. In April, more than 160 New York City businesses failed. People panicked, trying to regain losses and secure the safety of their money. They rushed to the bank to trade their paper money for precious metal. The bank run lasted two days in April and created a further economic disaster. New York City and the rest of the United States fell into a deep financial depression.

For the Blackwells, the nationwide financial panic of 1837 created a small-scale panic at home. The family had once hired many servants, enjoyed plenty of food, and had money to spend. Now, they faced ruin. Hannah and the three older girls took turns cooking. Elizabeth hated having to cook, saying:

This is my day for seeing to the meals, consequently I have not had much time for other things, I do really hate the employment, and look with real dread to my week [when I do the cooking].

Most meals included plenty of potatoes because they were so cheap. "We have become so poor ... we had no meat for dinner yesterday, today we had a stew composed of potatoes with a few bones," Elizabeth wrote. The Blackwells had no money for new clothes or shoes. Even candles were too expensive, so the family often went to bed at sunset. Anna took a teaching job in Vermont, and Marian and Elizabeth found work as governesses. The Blackwells' future looked bleak. ❖

As a young adult, Elizabeth found work as a teacher to help support her family. Before long, however, she would set her sights on a career in medicine.

CHAPTER THREE

LIFE CHANGES

In May 1838, Samuel moved his family to Ohio. The Blackwells sold what they could to pay for the trip, which they saw as a frontier adventure. At the time, Cincinnati was a rugged, pioneer town. It was a center of activity because it was situated on the Ohio River, a major shipping lane. Barges carried goods down to the Mississippi River and south or north to Cleveland and Lake Erie. The summer was exceptionally hot, and Samuel again became sick with malaria. On August 6, 1838, Elizabeth wrote in her diary:

He is dead. ... I had sat all the evening at the head of his bed with his right hand in mine how cold it was with the other I kept off the mosquitoes from him ... At 10 minutes past 10 he expired ... the burst of grief that proceeded from each one of us will never be forgotten.

Samuel left his family with less than $30. That was not even enough to feed them for a week. Everyone did their part to ensure the family's survival. Anna, Marian, and Elizabeth started a boarding school. Samuel Jr. took a job at the Cincinnati court-house. With hard work, the older children managed to support the younger ones and their mother, paying rent on a home and putting food on the table.

In 1842, the Blackwell sisters gave up the boarding school, which by this time was struggling to make money. Elizabeth taught private students. She was eventually offered a teach-ing job in Henderson, Kentucky, which was located down the Ohio River from Cincinnati. The town was not prepared to start

When Samuel Blackwell moved his family west to Cincinnati in 1838, he hoped it would be the start of a better life.

a school. Nor were they prepared for the steel will of young Elizabeth. She later recalled:

> *... the schoolhouse was hardly selected, the windows were broken, the floor and walls filthy ... the scholars unnotified of my arrival ... I urged and argued and persuaded and ran about, till a man was sent to mend the windows, and another to clean the floor ... and [responsible people] promised to collect the scholars, and on Monday I was to begin.*

A RUDE AWAKENING

Elizabeth had her first real encounter with slavery in Henderson. The Blackwell family had been openly opposed to slavery, but none of them had ever actually seen the practice in action. The difference between the lives of the owners and the lives of the slaves made a firm impression in Elizabeth's mind. She wrote:

> *I dislike slavery more and more everyday ... to live in the midst of beings degraded to the utmost in body and mind, drudging on from earliest morning to latest's night, cuffed about by everyone, scolded all day long, blamed unjustly, and ... to live in their midst utterly unable to help them, is to me dreadful.*

When Elizabeth's contract ended, she did not look for another job in Kentucky. She joined her family in their new home in Walnut Hill, on the outskirts of Cincinnati. The Lane Theological Seminary, a school for ministers, was close by. Elizabeth met

In Cincinnati, Elizabeth befriended the Beecher family (from l to r): Harriet Beecher Stowe, her father Lyman Beecher, and her brother Henry Ward Beecher.

and befriended Harriet Beecher Stowe and her family. One main topic of conversation among the friends was the anti-slavery movement. Elizabeth had a strong abolitionist background, and she found that her new friends felt the same way. Elizabeth grew to admire Stowe, who later wrote the popular anti-slavery novel *Uncle Tom's Cabin*.

Elizabeth also became friends with Mary Donaldson, a neighbor who was dying of cancer. Donaldson complained about the poor treatment she had received from male physicians and encouraged Elizabeth to become a doctor. "You are fond of study, have health and leisure; why not study medicine?" she asked her young friend. "If I could have been treated by a lady doctor, my worst sufferings would have been spared me."

When the idea was first presented, Elizabeth was totally against it. Yes, she was smart enough to learn medicine, but was it possible? Would she even want to study medicine when everything about the human body revolted her? "I had been always foolishly ashamed of any form of illness," she admitted.

At the time, there were no women doctors in the United States. There were no medical schools that accepted women. When Elizabeth asked her friends and family what they thought, she received little encouragement. She wrote to several doctors

Uncle Tom's Cabin

One of the most influential abolitionist books of the mid-1800s was Uncle Tom's Cabin, by Harriet Beecher Stowe. Stowe lived in Cincinnati for a time and saw firsthand the effects of slaveholding in Kentucky, which lay across the Ohio River. In 1850, she decided to write a book to protest slavery. Stowe's novel became the most sensational, influential, and best-selling book of the 19th century. In part, Uncle Tom's Cabin raised anti-slavery sentiments in the North and angered readers in the South. When President Abraham Lincoln met Stowe during the Civil War, he said, "So you're the little woman who wrote the book that started this Great War!"

Cincinnati: A Stop on the Underground Railroad

At the time Elizabeth lived there, Cincinnati was the Midwest center for the abolitionist movement. The city was a stop on the Underground Railroad that helped runaway slaves reach freedom in the North. Ohio was a free state, but it was not safe for runaways because it was so close to Kentucky. The Union Baptist Church provided a refuge and has documents that tell the story of the slaves who stayed there. The Allen Temple, Zion Baptist Church, and Wilson House also served as stations on the railroad.

and received the same message: It is a good idea but impossible. The two major obstacles were money and men. Medical school was expensive. Elizabeth had very little money, and her family could not help. Men dominated the medical profession. Even if Elizabeth found the money for school, she would need to convince those in authority to let her in. Still, she could not dismiss the idea of becoming a doctor. "The idea of winning a doctor's degree gradually assumed the aspect of a great moral struggle," she said years later, "and the moral fight possessed immense attraction for me."

Meanwhile, a new teaching job came open in Asheville, North Carolina. Elizabeth accepted the position and moved there in June 1845. She had been shocked by slavery in Kentucky, but

Elizabeth was appalled at the conditions in Asheville. Many people who invited Elizabeth into their homes owned slaves and treated them badly. After watching some women scold their slaves, Elizabeth wrote to her mother: "I longed to jump up, and taking the chains from those injured, unmanned men, fasten them on their tyrants till they learned ... the bitterness of [slavery]."

> **"I longed to jump up, and taking the chains from those injured, unmanned men, fasten them on their tyrants till they learned ... the bitterness of [slavery]."**
>
> – ELIZABETH BLACKWELL

Elizabeth decided she would do her best to help the children of slaves by teaching them to read and write—even though this was against the law. She tried to put her plan into action while teaching the slaves' children in Sunday school, but the ministers would not allow her to provide reading and writing lessons. Meanwhile, the whole time she was in Asheville, Elizabeth's thoughts kept returning to the idea of entering the medical profession. In fact, the idea had not left her mind since it was first introduced. While in Kentucky, she wrote in her journal, "I felt more determined than ever to become a physician." In her mind, medical school was no longer a question of *if*, but *when*. ❖

Elizabeth was rejected by many medical schools before being accepted by Geneva Medical College in upstate New York.

CHAPTER FOUR

THE FIRST WOMAN IN MEDICAL SCHOOL

REVEREND JOHN DICKSON CLOSED THE SCHOOL in Asheville in December 1845. He sent Elizabeth to stay with one of his relatives, Dr. Samuel Dickson, in Charleston, South Carolina. Elizabeth told Dr. Dickson about her desire to pursue medicine. He thought it was an excellent idea. Dickson, a highly respected doctor, even agreed to help her. Elizabeth spent hours pouring over the medical books in his huge library.

Dickson also found Elizabeth a job at his sister's boarding school. Although teaching provided an income, it did not make Elizabeth happy. In the fall, Elizabeth wrote to Emma Willard, a social reformer who promoted education for women. She believed Willard might be able to help her make useful connections. She needed to find male doctors willing to support the idea of a female doctor.

Emma Willard

Connecticut-born Emma Hart Willard (1787–1870) worked to help women become educated. In 1814, she opened her own school, the Middlebury Female Seminary, to

provide women with the chance to learn more about science, the arts, classical literature, and philosophy. Seven years later, she moved to Troy, New York, and opened the Troy Female Seminary. Willard supported a change in the roles women held in society. She believed that women were as intelligent as men and should have the right to an education equal to that given to men. She was the ideal person for Elizabeth Blackwell to contact about the possibility of going to medical school.

Through Willard, Elizabeth was introduced to Dr. Joseph Warrington. The Quaker doctor, who was practicing in Philadelphia, was well respected throughout the country. Warrington believed that only men should be doctors, but he saw no reason why women could not become nurses. Of course that wouldn't do for Elizabeth. She was determined to be a doctor. Nonetheless, Warrington would end up playing a part in helping Elizabeth reach her goal.

While in Philadelphia, Elizabeth took anatomy lessons at the private school of Dr. Allen. He helped her overcome her discomfort with the human body. Meanwhile, Elizabeth sought advice from many of Philadelphia's doctors about how to reach her goal of studying medicine. Some laughed. Others admired her determination.

A handful of doctors suggested that Elizabeth go to Paris to study. At the time, Paris was a center of medicine in Europe. It was known that some women disguised themselves as men to attend classes there. Warrington never changed his opinion about allowing women to become doctors, but he did agree to help Elizabeth. He used his contacts in the medical field and wrote letters of recommendation on her behalf.

TAKING THE NEXT STEP

Elizabeth wanted to be accepted to a medical school. She would need more than recommendations to make that happen. She would also need intelligence, patience, and determination. Elizabeth wrote to the top four medical schools in the country, including Harvard University, asking for a chance to study. Each one of the schools rejected her application. Elizabeth also applied to more than two dozen smaller schools. Finally, she was accepted to Geneva College in upstate New York. However, her acceptance was somewhat of an accident.

Dr. Warrington had written a letter of recommendation to Geneva about Elizabeth. The faculty did not want to insult

Warrington by rejecting her outright, so they came up with what they thought was a clever idea. They asked the students to vote on Elizabeth's acceptance, thinking they would say no. The students thought it was a joke and voted "aye." The faculty plan failed. Elizabeth Blackwell became the first woman accepted to an American medical college! "With an immense sigh of relief and aspiration of profound gratitude to Providence I instantly accepted the invitation [to attend Geneva], and prepared for the journey to Western New York State," she recalled.

Elizabeth left for Geneva on November 4, 1847. She traveled all night and arrived at 11 P.M. on November 6th. Elizabeth found lodging and registered for classes. Her boarding house

As soon as she received her acceptance letter, Elizabeth hurried to Geneva. She found a room in a boarding house not far from campus.

was a quick, three-minute walk from class. Elizabeth became student number 130, and she attended her first classes that same month. Classes were normally noisy and a bit unruly. Rather than raising their hands, students usually spoke out whenever they chose. A fellow student, Dr. Stephen Smith, later recalled the reaction to Elizabeth's first appearance in the classroom:

One morning, all unexpectedly, a lady entered the lecture-room with the professor; she was quite small of stature, plainly dressed, appeared diffident and retiring but had a firm and determined expression of face. Her entrance into that Bedlam of confusion acted like magic upon every student. Each hurriedly sought his seat … for the first time a lecture was given without the slightest interruption, and every word could be heard as distinctly as it would if there had been but a single person in the room.

Elizabeth was starting school late in the term. She had to scramble to catch up with her classmates. From the beginning, she was thrilled with the work. She later recalled:

[I] certainly have no reason to complain of medical students, for though they eye me curiously, it is also in a very friendly manner … I sometimes think I'm too much disciplined, but it is certainly necessary for the position I occupy. I believe the professors don't exactly know in what species of the human family to place me, and the students are a little bewildered.

Before Elizabeth began her studies, medical classes—including lessons in anatomy—were for men only.

Medical school cost $62 a term. Completion took at least two 16-week terms. Students had to learn about diseases and how to diagnose them. They also had to know all the parts of the human body. They learned about that in anatomy class, which had become one of Elizabeth's favorite subjects.

Professor of Anatomy James Webster eventually became Elizabeth's main supporter in the faculty. Early in her education, though, Webster told his only female student not to attend operations. The class was studying the reproductive system. The professor believed that discussing the material with a woman in class was not appropriate. This made Elizabeth angry. She wrote a note to Webster asking to be treated as an equal. "In this note,

I told him that I was there as a student with an earnest purpose, and as a student simply I should be regarded," she recalled. When Webster read the note to the class, they shouted their approval. From that time on, Elizabeth was considered as just one of the students—not just a woman student.

> **"I was there as a student with an earnest purpose, and as a student simply I should be regarded."**
>
> – ELIZABETH BLACKWELL

Elizabeth seemed to have the support of her fellow students. The women of Geneva were a different story. These ladies were not ready for a female medical student. Many women ignored her and most disapproved of her putting herself in direct compe-

A Woman's Role

In the 1800s, women's roles in life were clearly defined. Girls learned early that they would follow a predictable path: from daughter to wife to mother. When Elizabeth went to Geneva College, most states did not allow women to own property. Women could not vote, hold public office, or enter a profession. Women, it was believed, were weak and needed protection. Most women believed these ideas were true and did not want their roles in life to change. Geneva's women were like most other women of the time. They saw Elizabeth as a threat to their way of life and did not approve of what she was doing.

tition with men. Elizabeth wrote, "The ladies stopped to stare at me, as at a curious animal."

Slowly, Elizabeth changed the opinions of the men and women of both the school and the community. Professors came to admire her determination to succeed. She worked hard and earned excellent grades. The townsfolk also noticed that she was hardworking. Eventually they stopped treating her as an oddity. Dr. Charles Alfred Lee told Elizabeth:

> I'll venture to say in ten years' time one-third the classes in our college will consist of women. After the precedent you set, people's eyes will be open.

HOSPITAL WORK

Between the first and second terms, Elizabeth applied to work at Blockley Almshouse, a hospital for poor people in Philadelphia. Blockley was one of the largest hospitals in the United States. About 2,000 patients stayed there, many of whom had mental illnesses. Most were immigrants. The hospital also housed an orphanage, a poor house, and a drug store. A poor house provided housing for needy or dependent people and was usually paid for by public funds or taxes. The doctors at Blockley did not want to work with Elizabeth or let her watch them treat patients. The patients also complained. Once again, Elizabeth had to overcome other people's negative opinions of a woman doctor. Despite their

"When I walked into the wards [the doctors] walked out."

– ELIZABETH BLACKWELL

negativity, Elizabeth pushed to watch the doctors work with patients. "When I walked into the wards [the doctors] walked out," she wrote.

WOMEN'S RIGHTS ... OR NOT

During the summer of 1848, women's activists held a convention at Seneca Falls in upstate New York. It might seem that these women were working for the same things as Elizabeth—equality and opportunity for women. However, she did not want to get involved with their cause. Elizabeth did not want to get side-tracked from her own goal. She believed in achieving personal goals rather than working for group successes. She knew that

The Seneca Falls Convention, held in western New York State in 1848, brought people together to discuss the lack of rights for women in America.

she had worked for her achievements and thought that other women should do the same. They shouldn't rely on activists to fight for them, or the government to provide them with certain rights and privileges, she believed. She knew her own worth as a woman, yet Elizabeth didn't feel that all women were equally as talented or worthy.

Over the years, Elizabeth would often be asked to join women's causes and to work for women's rights. She rejected all invitations. Her work was solely in medicine. Although she helped other women in her field, Elizabeth was not interested in such ideas as women's voting or entering politics. She carved her own path and thought other women should do the same. Later in life, Elizabeth would meet many activists and suffrag-

Elizabeth Blackwell is probably the most famous graduate of Geneva Medical College. Today the school continues as the Hobart and William Smith Colleges.

ists, including her future sister-in-law Lucy Stone. Yet she never joined their movement.

In the fall, Elizabeth returned to Geneva to finish her studies. She earned top grades, which filled her fellow students with admiration. On January 23, 1849, Elizabeth graduated at the top of her class. She became the first female to earn a medical degree in the United States. Graduation was a step toward achieving her goal, but she still had more to learn.

After graduation, Elizabeth returned to Philadelphia temporarily. There, she became an official United States citizen. She planned to go to Europe and needed her citizenship before leaving the United States. As a citizen, she would not need to go through the process of immigration again and could leave and re-enter the United States easily. In Europe, Elizabeth hoped to study surgery and add to her medical knowledge. She was headed to Paris—the center of medical learning in Europe. ❖

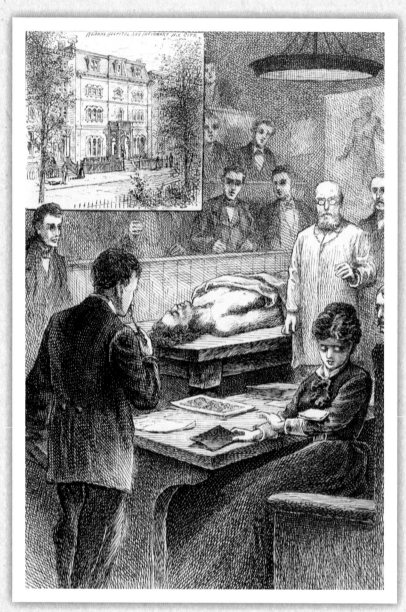

Elizabeth had to overcome her squeamish nature to study the human body and plan for a career in surgery.

CHAPTER FIVE

STUDIES ABROAD

I N THE SPRING OF 1849, ELIZABETH AND HER cousin Kenyon boarded a ship for Europe. England would be the first stop. The voyage was dreadful. Elizabeth was overwhelmed by seasickness for the first week. When the ship reached England on April 30, 1849, Elizabeth wrote:

Thanks be to Heaven, I am on land once more, and never do I wish again to experience that hideous nightmare—a voyage across the ocean.

Elizabeth spent several weeks in England before heading to Paris in May. Everything there was strange to her. She spent a lonely month until June, when her sister Anna arrived. The sisters toured the city and attended the theater together. Anna was so impressed by Paris that she decided to make it her home. It made Elizabeth happy to have family close by.

Elizabeth faced the same prejudices against women in Paris that she had in the United States—and more. The French medical community did not recognize her degree. Elizabeth asked to attend medical lectures and was refused. It didn't help that she did not speak French well. "I find I have much to learn," she said. "I have great trouble in expressing myself with any elegance, and I cannot see the physicians until I have acquired a tolerable command of words." It didn't take Elizabeth long to rectify the situation by learning French.

> "I find I have much to learn."
>
> – ELIZABETH BLACKWELL

A friend introduced Elizabeth to Doctor Pierre Louis, a famous Paris physician. Louis suggested she work at La Maternité, a large hospital where women gave birth and recuperated afterward. The situation at La Maternité was not what Elizabeth

Paris: A Medical Center

In the 1800s, medical studies in Paris were so advanced that doctors and students flocked there from America and other parts of Europe. It was a place where new medicine, research, and great advances in patient treatment took place. It was in Paris that Rene Laennec invented the stethoscope—a device that allowed doctors to listen to heartbeats—in 1816. Elizabeth Blackwell entered a thriving, active medical community.

La Maternité in Paris provided Elizabeth with a very good background in women's medicine.

hoped to find. She would not be working as a doctor, but as a student. Still, she decided to follow Louis's advice. Elizabeth wrote to her sister Marian about her decision:

I must enter La Maternité as [a student], be shut up for ... months without even stirring out for the laws are very strict and I suppose necessarily so for young French women and no exception can be made for me ... If I will consent to this imprisonment, I will be in the best school of midwifery in the world. In three months I shall witness 1,000 cases and be constantly practicing ... Will it not be worth the sacrifice and is it not wise to seize such an opportunity?

The students at La Maternité lived together in a large dormitory with 20 girls to a room. They were lively, noisy, and energetic. Elizabeth had a bed, a chair, and little else. Students were encouraged to work together. Many senior students helped teach the younger ones. They lived, studied, and ate together.

Students were not allowed to read anything other than medical textbooks. The day started at 5:30 A.M. The girls attended lectures and worked in the wards, which were large rooms shared by several patients. From 7 A.M. to 8 A.M., the headmistress, Madame Charrier, lectured to the girls. She quizzed the girls daily on what they learned. The day did not stop when the sun set. After a full day's work, many of the girls also had night duty in the wards. On her first turn at night duty, Elizabeth assisted with eight births. She found the harsh routine and lack of sleep during her internship tiring and difficult.

Elizabeth slowly earned the respect of her fellow students and doctors. Some even asked her for lessons on those subjects about which she knew more than they did. As it turned out, Elizabeth was both a student and a teacher at La Maternité. She later wrote about a particularly satisfying experience:

> *The other day, two of our chiefs begged me to give them a private lesson on the circulation of the blood … I explained to them what they did not know; they were very grateful, and have come to me several times since to beg me to continue my lesson …*

Elizabeth's time at La Maternité flew by. The days—and some nights—were filled with work. Elizabeth made friends with

Louis Pasteur was instrumental in the development of vaccines. Elizabeth's experiences with vaccination at La Maternité led her to speak out against the practice.

M. Hyppolyte Blot, a young doctor who asked her for lessons in English. Blot was the doctor in charge of vaccinations for the young babies. Several babies were vaccinated against smallpox at the same time. The students presented each baby, and the doctor cut the baby's skin with a knife. The vaccination process was crude and painful. Many of the vaccinated infants became seriously ill from the vaccine. Elizabeth connected at least one child's death directly to the child's being vaccinated.

TRAGEDY STRIKES

On November 4, 1849, Elizabeth was working in the infirmary when she came in contact with a baby who had an eye infection called purulent ophthalmia. Elizabeth picked up the infection in her eye. After examining her, Dr. Blot gave Elizabeth the bad news. "I learned from the tone of my friends that my eye was despaired of," she later wrote. "*Ah!* How dreadful it was to

"How dreadful ... to find the daylight gradually fading as my kind doctor bent over me."

– ELIZABETH BLACKWELL

find the daylight gradually fading as my kind doctor bent over me ... the sight soon vanished, and the eye was left in darkness."

The disease—and the treatments for the disease—were terribly painful. At the time of the infection, Elizabeth remained in bed for three weeks, slowly recovering her strength. Her right eye was still strong, but reading, writing, and any close work tired her. Over the months that followed, Elizabeth realized that this loss of sight was also the end of her dream. She had hoped to become a surgeon, which was the reason she had gone to Paris at the start. Now that was out of the question.

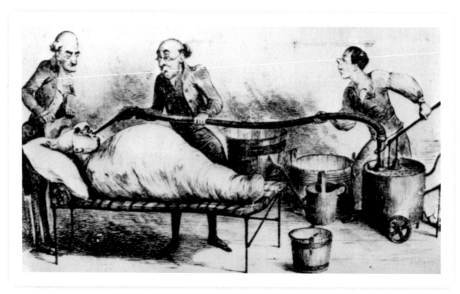

Not everyone thought hydrotherapy was a good idea—as evidenced by this cartoon, which mocks the practice of instructing patients to drink a lot of water.

Losing her eyesight stopped Blackwell from becoming a surgeon, but it would not stop her from practicing medicine. She was as determined as ever to set up a practice, but first she needed to regain her health.

TAKING THE WATERS

Elizabeth left La Maternité in June 1850 to recuperate. She went to Gräfenberg, in the Czech Republic, to a clinic run by Dr. Vincent Priessnitz, who promised to return her to health. Her therapy program consisted of a plain diet and water therapy. Hydrotherapy—water therapy—was a common medical practice in the 1800s. Patients took several baths, both hot and cold, followed by drinking large amounts of water throughout the day. Wet bandages were applied to the body.

Hydrotherapy

Sports medicine today uses ice packs, steam baths, and moving water (such as a whirlpool bath) to heal strained or injured muscles. These ideas came from Dr. Vincent Priessnitz, who developed the "Gräfenberg cure." Priessnitz insisted that his patients, including Elizabeth Blackwell, take advantage of water in every way. Patients had ice packs applied to their bodies. They also took both hot and cold plunge baths. Today, hydrotherapy helps treat burns, arthritis, spinal cord injuries, and bone injuries.

Elizabeth slowly regained her strength during two months of therapy. Then, her damaged eye became inflamed and had to be removed. She would need to wear a glass eye. Happily, at the end of the summer, Elizabeth received some good news from her cousin Kenyon. She would become a student at St. Bartholomew's Hospital in London. St. Bart's was one of the leading English hospitals, and many aspiring doctors wanted to work there. To be accepted as an intern was an honor.

GETTING BACK TO WORK

Elizabeth arrived in London in October 1850. She immediately set out for St. Bart's. She looked forward to becoming active in medicine again after her long illness and recovery. She said, "I was a quiet, sensible person who had acquired a small amount of medical knowledge and who wished by patient observation and study to acquire considerably more." At St. Bart's she would work with Dr. James Paget, who was a doctor and a teacher. Elizabeth found Paget's lessons interesting. Elizabeth's work at St. Bart's also included time working directly with patients. "I spend now about three or four hours each day in the wards," she said, "chiefly medical, diagnosing disease, watching the progress of cases, and accustoming my ear to the stethoscope."

Elizabeth found that every doctor and student welcomed her but one—the professor in charge of midwifery and women's diseases. Midwifery referred to the practice of delivering babies, which was also called obstetrics. The doctor had nothing particular against Elizabeth; he just did not think that women should study medicine.

Elizabeth attended only one regular lecture at St. Bart's. The head of students, Dr. James Paget, taught the course. Paget and his wife had become friends with Elizabeth, and he knew her medical qualifications. Elizabeth wrote in a letter, "Mr. Paget spoke to the students before I joined the class. When I entered and bowed, I received a round of applause. My seat is always reserved for me."

Although Elizabeth loved practicing medicine, she was lonely. She wanted to have professional relationships with other doctors with whom she could discuss medicine. She also began to think about setting up her own hospital where she could try new medical techniques. Elizabeth knew that her sister Emily was

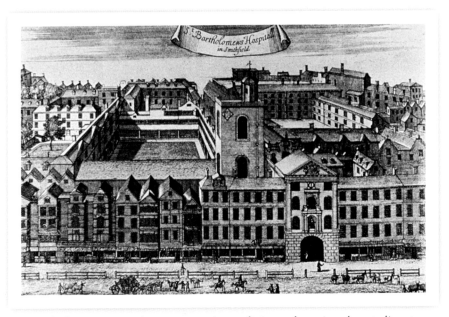

Elizabeth was given a chance to practice medicine and continue her studies at St. Bartholomew's Hospital in London.

interested in becoming a doctor. Elizabeth wrote to her about her plans for the future:

I shall commence as soon as possible building up a hospital in which I can experiment; and the very instant I feel sure of any improvement I shall adopt it in my practice. … If I were rich I would not begin private practice, but I would only experiment; as, however I am poor, I have no choice. I look forward with great interest to the time when you can aid me in these matters, for I have really no medical friend.

Medicine in the 1800s

In the 1800s, medicine was crude, inaccurate, and very often deadly. A hand on a forehead determined a fever because there were no thermometers. There was no way to take blood pressure. Doctors had no antibiotics or antiseptics in case of infection. Most doctors did not even know they should wash their hands between patients. Treatments for most diseases were different from those used today. For example, it was common for doctors to use bloodletting to treat fevers, headaches, flu, coughs, colds, and even toothaches. Bloodletting was done by cutting into a vein and draining out a small amount of blood. Another technique was to apply leeches to the patient's body to suck out blood.

After the Crimean War (1853–1856), Florence Nightingale became the second-best known woman in England after Queen Victoria.

MEETING FLORENCE NIGHTINGALE

Around this time, Elizabeth met a nurse named Florence Nightingale. The two spent many evenings together. They discussed problems dealing with the health of the poor, and sanitation in particular. Sanitation today means water and sewage systems, but in Elizabeth's time it meant cleanliness and hygiene. In the 1800s, few people realized the importance of bathing, washing their hands, or removing body waste in a safe way. This was true in homes and in hospitals. Both Elizabeth and Nightingale knew that many patients died from infections or diseases they caught because of poor sanitation. Elizabeth's interest in sanitation would increase in later life.

In three years, during the Crimean War, Nightingale would become involved in nursing. Just as Elizabeth was a pioneer in becoming a doctor, Nightingale paved the way for nursing to become a respected profession. Both women were intelligent,

Florence Nightingale: Founder of Modern Nursing

Florence Nightingale believed she had a calling to heal the sick. In 1854, Britain, France, and Turkey entered into the Crimean War against Russia. Nightingale answered the call to nurse the wounded. When she and 38 nurses first arrived at the military hospital near Istanbul they were ignored. At the time, nurses were male. Doctors did not want the help of women. As the number of wounded increased, however, female nursing became essential.

In 1860, Nightingale set up a school for nursing and helped establish professional nursing standards throughout Great Britain. In recognition of her work in promoting quality health care, Queen Victoria awarded Nightingale the Royal Red Cross in 1883. In 1907, Nightingale became the first woman to receive the British Order of Merit.

hardworking, and determined to succeed. Both fought prejudice against women in the medical field. Elizabeth admired Nightingale. She later wrote:

To her, chiefly, I owed the awakening to the fact that sanitation is the supreme goal of medicine, its foundation and its crown. ... When in later years, I entered into practice, extremely skeptical in relation to the value of drugs and ordinary medical methods, my strong faith in hygiene formed the solid ground from which I gradually built up my own methods of treatment.

Elizabeth paid her final visit to St. Bart's in July 1851. She was ready to return to the United States and put her medical knowledge to work. ❖

When Elizabeth returned to New York in 1851, she opened her own medical practice, but she had few patients at first.

CHAPTER SIX

Dr. Blackwell, Open for Business

ELIZABETH'S RETURN TO NEW YORK CITY WAS not the great success she had hoped it would be. Every hospital to which she applied rejected her. Someone suggested that she open her own doctor's office, and she did. Elizabeth had consulting rooms and medical knowledge, but no patients. With the help of newspaper editor Horace Greeley and an article he wrote in the *New York Tribune*, word spread that Dr. Blackwell was open for business. Patients slowly trickled in.

One of Elizabeth's early cases also helped ease her into the New York City medical world. She was treating an elderly woman with pneumonia and called in another doctor. She later wrote about the experience:

> *[The doctor] began to walk about the room in some*
> *agitation, exclaiming, 'A most extraordinary case! Such a*
> *one never happened to me before; I really do not know*

*what to do!' ... it was a clear case of pneumonia and of
no unusual degree of danger, until at last I discovered that
his perplexity related to me, not to the patient, and to the
propriety of consulting with a lady physician!*

The patient recovered, and the male doctor passed the word
that it was OK to work with Dr. Blackwell. More patients began
to find their way to her office. Despite her growing practice,
however, Elizabeth's days were far from full. She was terribly
lonely. She had few friends, no colleagues with whom to discuss
work, and no family in the area. Elizabeth had decided early in
her life that she would never marry. Four of her aunts did not
marry, nor did her sisters Anna, Marian, Ellen, and Emily. The
Blackwell women believed that few men were worth the loss of
personal freedom and independence that came with marriage.

THE INFIRMARY

To ease her loneliness, Elizabeth adopted a 7-year-old Irish girl
from the orphanage at Randall's Island. Katharine Barry, whom
Elizabeth called Kitty, filled the young doctor's life and chased
away her loneliness. Elizabeth wrote about her happiness with
Kitty in her journal:

*When I took her to live with me, she was about seven
and a half years old. I desperately needed the change
of thought she compelled me to give her. It was a dark
time, and she did me good—her genial, loyal, Irish
temperament suited me.*

Meanwhile, Emily Blackwell had decided to follow her sister into medicine. Elizabeth warned her that she would face resistance if she became a doctor, but Emily would not be discouraged. Like her sister, Emily had some trouble finding the right school. She began her training at Rush Medical School in Chicago, but left when the doctor who served as her patron left the school. Emily headed to Cleveland, Ohio, where she earned a medical degree from Western Reserve University's medical school in 1854.

Randall's Island Orphanage

Randall's Island is located in New York's East River. At various times it has housed a cemetery for the poor, a poor house, a home for juvenile delinquents, a mental hospital, and an orphanage. The orphanage at Randall's Island was one of several in New York City at the time that Elizabeth adopted Kitty.

Most of the children at Randall's Island came from Russian, German, or Irish immigrant families. Often their parents could not find work and could not afford to feed them. Sometimes, their mothers died in childbirth and there was no one else to care for them. The orphanage was run by New York City and paid for with tax money. Few laws controlled the adoption process until the 1850s. Before then, anyone interested in adopting a child simply went to the orphanage, made a selection, and signed the papers.

Emily spent the nine months between terms studying in New York, where she and Elizabeth planned to open a clinic. The women launched the New York Dispensary for Poor Women and Children in March 1854. The Blackwells chose the location of their clinic to be close to poor immigrant women who needed help. Elizabeth's interest in improved sanitation became an important service of the clinic. She spent six hours a week offering advice on hygiene, cleanliness, healthy food, and fresh air. The money to run the dispensary came from Quaker supporters. Without their help, the Blackwell clinic would have closed its doors soon after it opened.

In 1854, Elizabeth helped Marie Zakrzewska get her medical education. Zakrzewska had been a midwife in Europe and had an excellent medical background. She had the same intelligence and determination as the Blackwell sisters. After finishing her education, Zakrzewska joined the Blackwells in New York.

Dr. Emily Blackwell joined her sister Elizabeth in opening the New York Infirmary for Women and Children.

The Society of Friends

In the 1700s and 1800s, Quakers, also known as the Society of Friends, made up one-third of New York City's population. The Quakers held the progressive attitude that women and men should be treated equally. They had women preachers, which was unusual at the time. Quakers supported women's voting, property rights, and entry into politics. Because of their strong beliefs in favor of women, it is no surprise that many of the New Yorkers who helped Elizabeth were Quakers.

THE NEW YORK INFIRMARY

Elizabeth's plan from the beginning had been to open a full-fledged hospital. She had the charter that set up the clinic, and a board of directors to help with organization. The only thing the women needed to turn the clinic into a hospital was money, which they got by requesting contributions from everyone they knew. The three women rented a house at 64 Bleecker Street in one of the worst slums in Manhattan. The location was chosen because the area had no hospital or doctors, and the people were too poor to find medical care elsewhere.

The women opened the New York Infirmary for Women and Children on May 12, 1857. Elizabeth served as the director. Emily was the clinic's surgeon, and Dr. Marie Zakrzewska was the resident physician. They ran a hospital for women, staffed entirely by women. At the time, male doctors and nurses made up 99 percent of the medical profession. For a woman to be able to go to a female doctor was unusual. To go to a hospital run only by women was not possible.

Clearly, women had been waiting for such an opportunity. The infirmary was a success. Within a month, all beds were full and dozens of patients showed up at the outpatient clinic. Women and children who had no money got free medical care. Those with money paid $4 a week. In the first eight months, the infirmary treated 866 patients.

Manhattan's Slums

In 1850, nearly 700,000 people lived in New York City. The fast-growing population had doubled in just 10 years, putting a strain on the city. Apartment buildings sprang up and were crowded next to each other to house all the new residents. Immigrants joined friends, families, and fellow countrymen in these small neighborhoods. Many of the areas were overcrowded, and the buildings were poorly maintained. The people lived in squalor. The most notorious neighborhood was called Five Points. It was named for the spot where five streets—Mulberry, Little Water, Anthony, Cross, and Orange—met. Five Points was mainly made up of Irish families, although there were also many African Americans and Italians. The people who lived in these slum neighborhoods became Elizabeth's patients.

One of Elizabeth's hopes for the infirmary was to start a medical college for women. She and Emily both planned to teach in the school.

As might be expected, there were many who spoke against the idea of a hospital run by women. They spread gossip and rumors that the Blackwells and Zakrzewska were immoral women who should not be trusted. Both men and women spoke out against them. When a woman died giving birth, protesters held a demonstration outside the hospital. The angry crowd grew, and the police showed up to bring the situation under control.

Elizabeth continued seeing patients, but she also had other interests. She began giving lectures about the education of girls and improved hygiene. She felt strongly that many of her patients got sick because they did not bathe, eat good food, or live in clean homes. The lectures were well received. Elizabeth made plans for giving more lectures, as well as having them published.

THE SUFFRAGISTS COME CALLING

Once again, the women's rights movement wanted Elizabeth to take an interest in their activities. Elizabeth's brother Henry, his wife Lucy Stone, Elizabeth Cady Stanton, and Susan B. Anthony were active suffragists. They felt that Elizabeth might be drawn in because of her relationship to Henry and Lucy, but Elizabeth held fast to her beliefs. She may have thought that some women could live up to the responsibility of voting, but she did not think women as a whole should have the right to vote. "I believe that

Lucy Stone

Lucy Stone (1818–1893) was a prominent American suffragist and anti-slavery reformer. In 1855, Stone married Elizabeth's brother, abolitionist Henry Brown Blackwell. She shocked many people by refusing to take her husband's last name as her own. She also opposed many of the common laws that controlled married women of her time. Well-educated and independent minded, Stone helped form the American Equal Rights Association, with the goal of establishing equal voting rights for both genders and all races. Lucy and Henry also helped found the American Woman Suffrage Association.

the chief source of the false position of women is the inefficiency of women themselves," she said. "The deplorable fact is that they are so often careless mothers, weak wives, poor housekeepers, ignorant nurses, and frivolous human beings." Even Lucy Stone could not change such a strong opinion.

A RETURN TO ENGLAND

In August 1858, Elizabeth returned to England with her daughter Kitty. She told Emily, "I am so tired of physical privations that it does seem to me I would rather work where I could make [the] most money and have good food and clothes and that I think would be in London."

While in England, Elizabeth met again with Florence Nightingale—now one of the most famous women in Great Britain. Her efforts to help British soldiers in the Crimean War were legendary. Nightingale wanted to start a nursing school and hoped that Elizabeth would run it.

> **"The deplorable fact is that [women] are so often careless mothers, weak wives, poor housekeepers, ignorant nurses, and frivolous human beings."**
>
> – ELIZABETH BLACKWELL

Elizabeth was a doctor. In fact, she became the first woman doctor to have her name placed on the British medical register in 1859. She had no interest in getting involved in Nightingale's nursing school. Elizabeth wanted to open a women's hospital in England similar to the New York Infirmary. Elizabeth liked England and hoped that she and Kitty could settle there permanently, but she needed to work. A women's hospital would

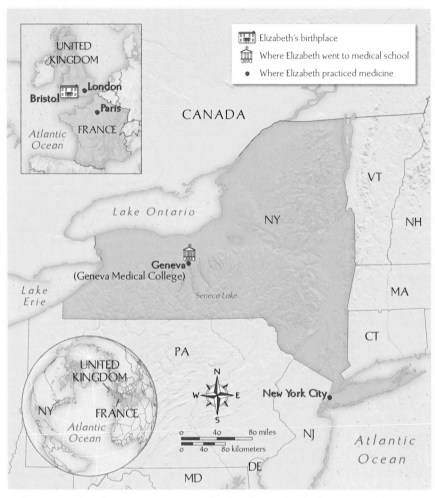

After earning her degree at Geneva Medical College, Elizabeth continued her studies in Paris and London. She set up a practice in New York City before returning once again to England, where she lived for the rest of her life.

provide that opportunity. Elizabeth wanted to work with Nightingale, but not if she had to run a school for nurses' training. She wrote, "[Nightingale] wishes, I see, to absorb me in this nursing plan which would simply kill me, if it did not accomplish my medical plan." British doctors were practical. They saw that the public favored Nightingale, so they sided with her, too. Elizabeth would not get any support for her idea of opening a women's hospital. After a year away, Elizabeth decided to return to the United States and her work at the infirmary. ❖

When the Civil War began, Elizabeth began training women as nurses to help care for the wounded.

CHAPTER SEVEN

THE CIVIL WAR ERA

O N A WARM APRIL DAY IN 1861, THE NEWLY formed Confederate Army fired on Fort Sumter in Charleston Harbor. That act began the American Civil War (1861–1865), a contest that pitted North against South. The war quickly expanded from this one event to major battles. With the battles came many wounded.

Elizabeth began working for the war effort immediately. Despite her disagreements with Florence Nightingale, Elizabeth admired what Nightingale had done to ease suffering during the Crimean War. She decided to use some of Nightingale's ideas to help the North win the Civil War.

Two weeks after the firing on Fort Sumter, Elizabeth held a meeting at the infirmary. About 50 women attended. They planned to collect money and supplies for wounded soldiers and sailors. They would collect canned foods, blankets, socks, books, and writing paper. They also planned to train nurses. Elizabeth became one of the major organizers of the Women's Central Relief Association (WCRA). Four thousand people attended the first major meeting of the WCRA.

BRINGING RELIEF

The women of the WCRA were excellent organizers. They realized they needed to have a central depot for collecting and distributing supplies. They also needed someone to arrange the nurses' training program. They chose Elizabeth Blackwell for the job. The WCRA evolved into the U.S. Sanitary Commission and was officially accepted by the War Department at the suggestion of President Abraham Lincoln.

The Sanitary Commission, an off-shoot of Elizabeth's Civil War work, promoted healthier conditions in military camps—and helped save many lives.

Sanitary Fairs

Throughout the Civil War, volunteers held Sanitary Fairs to earn money to buy needed supplies for the wounded. The Women's Central Relief Association, originally organized by Elizabeth Blackwell, participated in Sanitary Fairs. People paid admission to tour exhibits that included art, furniture, musical instruments, toys, and even flowers. Visitors could also buy the exhibited items at an auction. One of the most practical items auctioned was a shipload of coal. The most unusual may have been a tame bear.

The first successful Sanitary Fair was held in Chicago. It earned nearly $100,000 (more than $2 million in today's dollars)—a fact that encouraged other Union (Northern) cities to hold fairs

The Sanitary Fair held in New York City in 1864 was one of the most successful.

of their own. The two most successful events were the Philadelphia and New York City fairs. Each city raised about $1 million (almost $25 million today), which went toward purchasing everything from bandages to writing paper to socks—whatever wounded soldiers needed.

Elizabeth began training women to be nurses at New York's Bellevue Hospital in 1861. She and her committee carefully reviewed an endless pile of applications to choose the women they believed would make good nurses. The 91 women selected would attend a one-month training program before being sent to Army hospitals. Once there, they had to deal with the prejudices of the U.S. Army. Although the Army was grateful for the bandages, cakes, and other goods collected by the Sanitary Commission, they did not want female nurses. Up to this time, nursing was a job for males only. Any women who worked in hospitals were considered low class and immoral.

Eventually, the sheer number of casualties forced those in charge to reconsider their opinions. The Army needed more nurses, and there weren't enough men available. It was as simple as that. The government had to set up an official training program. Dorothea Dix was chosen to head up the Sanitary Commission nursing program. Despite Elizabeth's efforts on behalf of the nursing program, the government had overlooked her when choosing a leader. The reason behind this decision was political. Dix had powerful friends; Elizabeth did not. Elizabeth stepped back and had to follow Dix's directions. Dix insisted that the women chosen for the program had to be 30 to 45 years old. They needed to be strong, honest, trustworthy, and hard-working. They also needed to be plain looking, and they could not wear hoops in their skirts. (Wide skirts would get in the way as nurses tried to move between patients.)

One of the major efforts of the Sanitary Commission was promoting hygiene in army camps, an idea that had Elizabeth's

Dorothea Dix

Dorothea Dix (1802–1887) worked to reform mental asylums in the United States, England, and Scotland. In the 1800s, patients in mental hospitals were held in cages and chains. With the help of

newspaper editor Horace Greeley and educator Horace Mann, Dix convinced states to pass laws that demanded kinder treatment for mental patients. In 1861, the U.S. Army appointed Dix to be the head of nurses' training during the Civil War. Many people thought Elizabeth Blackwell should have been chosen, but Dix held the job throughout the war. After the war ended, Dix returned to her efforts to improve health care for mentally ill people.

full support. During the war, nearly half of all deaths were not caused by bullets, bombs, or cannonballs but by diarrhea, dysentery, typhoid fever, and stomach disorders. Many soldiers also caught diseases that are rare in today's society, such as measles, mumps, chickenpox, whooping cough, pneumonia, and tuberculosis. The last two also led to many deaths.

One of Elizabeth's most satisfying experiences during the Civil War was meeting President Abraham Lincoln. She traveled to Washington, D.C., toured the city, and visited the White House, where she was invited to visit with the president. "A tall ungainly loose-jointed man was standing in the middle of the room," she later wrote. "He came forward with a pleasant smile and shook hands with us. I should not at all have recognized him from the photographs." It was Lincoln. After the visit, Blackwell spent time with Dorothea Dix to discuss nurses' training.

THE WOMEN'S MEDICAL COLLEGE

As the war dragged on, Elizabeth turned her attention to a new project. In December 1863, she spoke to a number of supporters about building a medical school for women. By this time, a handful of female students had been accepted into men's colleges, but they were still considered odd. The women's medical schools that had opened offered their students poor educations. Elizabeth wanted to start a new medical college for women that would be superior to its competition.

Elizabeth got advice from other doctors and medical professors about how to set up and manage the school. She even decided on the classes that would be held and the rules for running the school. It would be several years before the college could accept students, though. The Blackwells worked hard to find the money to build the school, the people to run it, and the teachers to lead classes. The sisters also worked in the infirmary and continued their work for the war effort. Although they worked together constantly, Elizabeth and Emily were not getting along.

Thanks to Elizabeth's pioneering work, more women began attending medical schools, such as the Women's Medical College of Pennsylvania, located in Philadelphia.

Elizabeth had endless trouble with her remaining eye. The eye tired easily, and Elizabeth could not do any close work. Though she rarely complained, Elizabeth grew frustrated by these limitations. Once she admitted:

My eyes [are] so much weakened that I dare neither read a book, nor write a lecture. The sight is perfect but the eye becomes fatigued with any continued exertion and the reading of even a chapter in a book is quite out of the question.

Elizabeth was a driven person, and the difficulty of doing simple jobs or studying new medical ideas was frustrating. Emily was not as driven as her sister. She was not terribly interested in medicine and had become bored with surgery. It was not easy for the sisters to work together. Emily thought Elizabeth was bossy, and Elizabeth thought Emily lacked determination. Still, Elizabeth decided to put their differences aside until the college was up and running.

The Women's Medical College of the New York Infirmary opened on November 2, 1868. The teaching staff included both men and women, and Elizabeth made sure that all teachers were at the top of their fields. The students had to take a three-year course of study—one year longer than the normal medical school requirements. They would also be examined by a group of doctors from outside the school. No one would ever question the skills of any doctor who graduated from the Women's Medical College. When the school opened, Elizabeth was the

Kitty truly was a blessing to Elizabeth. Aside from a few short separations, mother and daughter were constant companions throughout Elizabeth's life.

professor of hygiene. Hygiene and sanitation had been one of her major interests since she first met Florence Nightingale in 1851. The school was an immediate success. Elizabeth felt that now her work in America was finished. She left Emily in charge of the school and the hospital and returned to England.

By this time Kitty was in her early twenties. The young woman had an interesting relationship with her mother—and the rest of Elizabeth's family. As much as she loved Kitty, Elizabeth sometimes treated her like a personal ser-

> **"That child has been, and is, so great a blessing to me, that I hardly know what I should have done without her."**
>
> – ELIZABETH BLACKWELL

vant. For most of her life, Kitty did not use the Blackwell name, and she called her Blackwell relatives by rather formal titles, such as "Mr. Henry" or "Dr. Emily." Elizabeth once said about Kitty, "That child has been, and is, so great a blessing to me, that I hardly know what I should have done without her." Yet, Elizabeth returned to England without her daughter.

Elizabeth entered a new stage of her life alone. She would not practice medicine in England herself, but that would not stop her from helping other women succeed in the medical field. ❖

After returning to Great Britain in 1869, Elizabeth decided to make her home there permanently.

CHAPTER EIGHT

Pioneer Work

B Y 1869, WOMEN IN THE UNITED STATES HAD taken great strides in the medical profession. There were several medical schools for women and several hundred women doctors. The same was not true in Great Britain, where women still had trouble getting into medical school. Elizabeth planned to return to England and try to change that. Two British women whom she knew well were already making headway: Elizabeth Garrett Anderson and Sophia Jex-Blake.

Elizabeth Blackwell had met Garrett Anderson in 1859 and inspired her to pursue a medical career. Garrett Anderson could not find a medical school in England that would accept her. However, she discovered that she could enter the medical profession by taking an exam given by the Society of Apothecaries. The society wanted to refuse the young lady's request to take the exam, but her father threatened to sue them. Garrett Anderson

Elizabeth Garrett Anderson was able to become a doctor by passing the apothecaries' exam.

took the test and passed. Within a year she was registered as a medical doctor.

Sophia Jex-Blake had been a student of Blackwell's medical school in New York. In 1869, Jex-Blake entered Edinburgh University in Scotland. The next year, while she was supposed to be taking an anatomy test, a group of students assembled outside the classroom to protest the presence of women in their school. The situation drew the interest of local newspapers. Jex-Blake became involved in the protests and newspaper interviews. She missed some exams and failed others. Bad-tempered and outspoken, she accused the doctors giving the exams of being against her and failing her on purpose. The doctors were well respected in Edinburgh. So in the end, her actions hurt the cause of women in medicine.

Though they disapproved of her actions, Blackwell and Garrett Anderson gave Jex-Blake another chance. They let her join them as they set up the London School of Medicine for Women. Dr. Blackwell became the professor of hygiene. Dr. Garrett Anderson taught about women's diseases.

Elizabeth Garrett Anderson

Although Elizabeth Blackwell had been accepted as a doctor in England, Elizabeth Garrett Anderson (1836–1917) was the first woman to be officially approved to practice medicine in Great Britain. A pioneer in the medical field, Garrett Anderson was born in Aldeburgh, England, and had nine brothers and sisters. The Garretts believed in a full education for their children. They encouraged Elizabeth to study Latin and math with her brothers. In 1859, she met Elizabeth Blackwell when Dr. Blackwell was giving a series of lectures in London. Like Blackwell, Garrett Anderson struggled to get a medical education. After passing the exam given by the Society of Apothecaries, her name was added to the Medical Register—the official list of qualified doctors. In 1866, she opened the St. Mary's Dispensary for Women. In 1871, she married James Anderson. The following year she opened the New Hospital for Women and Children.

Opened in 1874, the school provided a medical education to 14 female students. Elizabeth kept her eye on Jex-Blake. Just after the school opened, Dr. Blackwell wrote to a friend:

I am very busy about the Medical College in the delicate work of reorganizing the affair and securing proper safeguards against the headlong energies of its most active member [Sophia Jex-Blake] … We shall always have a certain amount of trouble with Miss J.B. but things look rather promising for getting sufficient controlling force to keep her cleverness and energy in their proper place. I have been obliged to work single handed in this matter of cautioning our Council and securing certain measures, for Mrs. Anderson has too much on hand … But all are working harmoniously.

By this time, Elizabeth had spent several months in England alone. Her 22-year-old daughter Kitty remained in the United

Once Elizabeth decided to stay in England, Kitty joined her. Mother and daughter (shown here around 1905 with their dogs) lived together for the rest of Elizabeth's life.

States, and Elizabeth missed her terribly. Despite maintaining a medical practice, lecturing at the London medical school, and all her other interests, Elizabeth was lonely.

Elizabeth had originally planned to return to the United States. When she made up her mind to stay permanently in England, she asked Kitty to join her.

THE RELIGION OF HEALTH

In 1869, Elizabeth gave a lecture to the Working Women's College titled "How to Keep a Household in Health." The lecture dealt with ways to keep a home clean and prevent disease. Health and hygiene continued to be Elizabeth's main interests. She believed in medical treatment for disease, but she also thought that many diseases could be prevented by cleanliness and a good diet. She also believed in water therapy. All these ideas, Elizabeth believed, should be applied to normal medical care. She thought doctors and nurses should learn as much about the value of hygiene to prevent disease as they knew about medicines or surgery. "Our hospitals and dispensaries need to promote practical hygiene," she said. "Our medical schools should turn the force of their learning, ability, and great influence to the conversion of their students into a vast body of sanitary missionaries."

> **"Our medical schools should turn the force of their learning, ability, and great influence to the conversion of their students into a vast body of sanitary missionaries."**
>
> – ELIZABETH BLACKWELL

In the late 1880s, disease was widespread in London. Elizabeth hoped to reduce the rate of sickness and death by promoting hygiene.

Elizabeth studied the death rate of Londoners to find out the causes of most deaths in that city. She found that the death rate for children was particularly high. Elizabeth knew she had a solution, though. She believed that women doctors could promote better health through hygiene. She said:

> *Year by year the [death rate] might be lessened by the sanitary knowledge [spread] by women, and the sanitary regulations their influence might establish, until from their own little circle they could look with joy to a bright cloud of witnesses beyond—thousands of useful lives saved to their homes and country through their aid!*

CHANGES IN MEDICINE

From the 1880s to the end of her life, Elizabeth found it hard to keep up with medical advances. She was no longer practicing medicine herself, nor did she go back to school to learn new medical ideas and techniques. Elizabeth also continued to have trouble with her eye, which made reading difficult. Some of the changes that were taking place shocked her; others disappointed her. Among the ideas that she found most difficult to accept were germ theory, vivisection, and vaccinations.

Germ theory proposed that small organisms in the body caused diseases. Elizabeth placed her medical beliefs in hygiene, diet, and quality of life. She could not accept that tiny living things traveled through the air, entered human bodies, and made people sick. No amount of scientific proof changed her mind.

Elizabeth's anger over vivisection was even stronger. She did not like the idea of making animals sick so doctors and scientists could try new medicines on them. In 1889, when she was in her late sixties, Elizabeth visited renowned scientist Louis Pasteur in his laboratory. He kept many live animals—rabbits, dogs, guinea pigs, and pigeons—for use in his experiments. At the time, he was trying to find medical solutions to anthrax and rabies.

Seeing the painful condition of several of the dogs upset Elizabeth. The situation seemed particularly cruel to her because she couldn't see any connection between animal anatomy and that of humans. She was quick to point out that a dog's body, organs, and blood were not like human bodies, organs, or blood.

Elizabeth was so opposed to vivisection that she wrote to her sister Emily, now the dean of the New York Infirmary Medical

Vivisection

Vivisection literally means the cutting of live animals. In the medical field, vivisection refers to a variety of experiments that are performed on live animals. There is a long history of student doctors' cutting up pigs, sheep, or dogs to study the body parts. By the 1800s, doctors used many animals to study human diseases or test the effectiveness of new vaccines. Elizabeth Blackwell strongly opposed this idea. She said that animal bodies had nothing in common with human bodies and could not be useful in medical studies.

Elizabeth was very much opposed to vivisection, though it was a common practice in the 19th century.

School. She said that if the school was using vivisection as a teaching tool, it was to stop immediately. She even threatened to return to New York to put an end to the practice if necessary.

Elizabeth saw vaccinations as equally evil. She had a bad experience with the practice. The British government had passed a law that required all children to be vaccinated against small-pox. While the idea was a good one for general public health,

Elizabeth believed it caused needless deaths. When she was a student at La Maternité, one of Elizabeth's patients had become sick and died after she vaccinated him.

Elizabeth spoke out against the practice, but modern medical thinking won out. Many well-known doctors believed that vaccinations were essential to stopping epidemics.

IN HER OWN WORDS

When she was in her seventies, friends convinced Elizabeth to write her autobiography. She called the book *Pioneer Work in Opening the Medical Profession to Women*. It was far more interesting than the title might suggest. The book covered Elizabeth's life from childhood on, and she fleshed out the chapters with copies of documents, letters, and her own journal entries. *Pioneer Work in Opening the Medical Profession to Women* showed Elizabeth's intelligence, dedication, and sense of humor.

In the book, Elizabeth looked back on her successes and the difficulties in being a pioneer. In it, she wrote:

> *Though a woman may now become a legally qualified practitioner of medicine, the task is still a very arduous one. ... There is a noble and useful life to be gained by the conquest of these difficulties, but ... they require perseverance, courage, and self-reliance.* ❖

Elizabeth and her daughter Kitty (pictured) lived in Rock House in Hastings, a short train ride from London.

CHAPTER NINE

A LIFE WELL SPENT

I N 1879, ELIZABETH AND KITTY MOVED TO ROCK House in Hastings (near London), where Elizabeth lived for the next 31 years. There, Elizabeth organized the Moral Reform Union. The job of this group was to make sure local young people behaved according to social ideals of the times. The group became involved in local politics, which gave Elizabeth the idea that women might succeed in running a small town. In that role, they could encourage the decent behavior of citizens.

Elizabeth was asked to run for Poor Law Guardian. She lost the election, which was something of a relief. She had no interest in dealing with ordinary citizens every day, and less interest in working directly with the poor. This was a surprising attitude from someone who had been poor much of her life and who faced poverty in her old age. (Elizabeth's books were interesting and well written, but they did not earn much profit.)

THE PIONEER'S LAST DAYS

At the turn of the century, Elizabeth was nearly 80 years old. Many of her family and friends had died, and her own health was poor. Her family, large as it was, was fast disappearing. Elizabeth's sister Marian had died in 1897. In 1900, sister Anna passed on as well. The following year brought the deaths of both Ellen and Sam Blackwell.

In 1901, Elizabeth's brother Henry asked her to make a visit to the United States. Despite the fact that she hated sea travel, Dr. Blackwell crossed the Atlantic at age 80. Much had changed during her lifetime. The voyage that had once taken months was completed in a few weeks. Elizabeth visited her family in Martha's

When Elizabeth (seated, in hat) returned to the United States for a visit, the Blackwell family gathered in Martha's Vineyard, Massachusetts.

Vineyard, Massachusetts. She also had the chance to ride in a car—a fun and novel experience. The trip was delightful.

Once they returned to England, Elizabeth and Kitty stayed in Hastings with the exception of a yearly vacation to Kilmun, Scotland. It was there in 1907 that Elizabeth suffered a serious fall. Injury and age proved to be too much for her to overcome. For the next three years, Kitty nursed her mother as Elizabeth's health continued to fail.

> **"She was in the fullest sense of the word a pioneer who, like all pioneers [when discouraged] heard but did not listen."**
>
> – THE LONDON TIMES

In 1910, Elizabeth suffered a stroke. She died on May 31. Obituaries were published in newspapers across Great Britain and the United States. The *London Times* wrote: "She was in the fullest sense of the word a pioneer who, like all pioneers [when discouraged] heard but did not listen." People suggested building memorials in Dr. Blackwell's honor. Those closest to her knew Elizabeth would not have wanted that. Her legacy could never be a slab of stone. It is, instead, the living women who were succeeding in medicine when she died.

THE ELIZABETH BLACKWELL AWARD

In the 1950s, Hobart and William Smith Colleges (formerly Geneva College) founded the Elizabeth Blackwell Award. The award is given to honor women who have offered outstanding service to humanity. Two aspects of Elizabeth's own life guide the choices of the award winners. Dr. Blackwell opened doors to other women. She also lived a life of service, using her talents and skills to help others. Women who receive the Elizabeth Blackwell Award have achieved some level of greatness in their work and have helped others in some way.

Over the years, the award has been given to several doctors, including Helen Taussig and Antonia Novello. Recipients include women who have paved the way in other fields, as well. Tennis star and women's rights activist Billie Jean King received the award because she worked to gain equal pay and respect for women athletes. Sandra Day O'Connor, another winner, was the first female justice of the U.S. Supreme Court. The committee that determines the winners also chose Wilma Mankiller, the first woman chief of the Cherokee tribe. Female government offi-

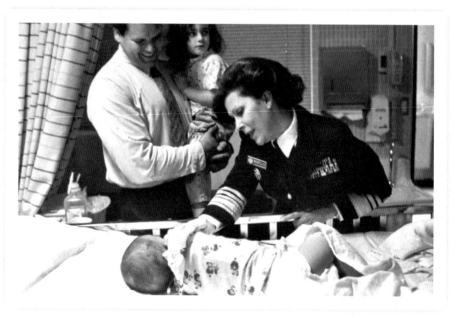

In 1990, Dr. Antonia Novello was appointed Surgeon General of the United States. She was the first woman, and the first Latin American, to hold the post.

Helen Taussig, M.D.

Helen Taussig (1898–1986) was the first woman to become the president of the American Heart Association and is considered the founder of pediatric (children's) cardiology. She was honored many times for her work on "blue baby syndrome." This condition describes a baby born with a heart condition that makes the baby look blue due to a lack of oxygen. When she graduated from Johns Hopkins University School of Medicine, Taussig had already lost her hearing. She relied on lip-reading and hearing aids throughout her career. So acute was her sense of touch that she was able to distinguish the rhythms of normal and damaged hearts by feel. In addition to the Elizabeth Blackwell Award, she also received the Medal of Freedom, from President Lyndon Johnson. Taussig was also the first woman to hold a full professorship at Johns Hopkins University School of Medicine.

cials Madeleine Albright (the first female Secretary of State) and U.S. Senator Margaret Chase Smith have also won the Elizabeth Blackwell Award.

THE LEGACY CONTINUES

When the Blackwells founded the New York Infirmary for Women and Children, they could not have imagined their creation surviving more than 10 years, let alone more than 150. They scraped together just enough money to open the medical center, and they kept scrambling for money year after year.

In 1979, Beekman Downtown Hospital and the New York Infirmary joined together to form the NYU Downtown Hospital. Today, the hospital serves several million people. It is the closest emergency care facility for Lower Manhattan's employees, residents, and visitors. As the first facility to answer nearly every medical emergency in Lower Manhattan, New York Downtown Hospital treats more than 30,000 emergency patients yearly.

Answering the Call

When the terrorist attack on New York City's World Trade Center occurred on September 11, 2001, NYU Downtown Hospital was the closest hospital to ground zero. Doctors and nurses there treated as many as 175 patients an hour. According to Dr. Bruce Logan, "The cafeteria was filled with people on 9/11. There were hundreds of people seen that day in the cafeteria alone." Based on that experience, hospital administrators decided to build a new $25 million emergency department. They would be ready to handle any major emergencies in the future.

If Elizabeth Blackwell were alive today, she would look at the changes in medicine with amazement. Since she began practicing medicine in 1851, thousands of medical advances have taken place. Antibiotics help cure infections. Diseases such as whooping cough, polio, and measles are rare because of vaccinations that prevent those diseases. Surgery is performed in the morning, and the patient goes home in the afternoon.

The role of women in medicine has also changed. In 2006, the United States had more than 256,000 female doctors. That number continues to grow. The American Medical Association (AMA) once refused to allow women membership. Today the organization has a Women Physicians Congress (WPC), which represents more than 63,000 female physicians and medical students. Two of WPC's goals are to increase the number, voice, and influence of women physicians and to promote women's health issues. Today, 16 percent of the world's scientists are women. There was only a mere handful in the 1850s. Just over 27 percent of doctors are women, and women make up nearly half of all medical students.

Elizabeth once said, "What is done or learned by one class of women becomes, by virtue of their common womanhood, the property of all women." Her pioneering efforts forced open the doors to medicine for all women. Even she could not have imagined the flood of women who would follow and the legacy she would leave behind. Elizabeth's legacy does not just encompass women doctors, it touches every women who strives to succeed in her chosen field. ❖

TIME LINE

1821 Elizabeth Blackwell is born on February 3 in Bristol, England.

1832 The Blackwells emigrate to the United States and settle in New York.

1838 The Blackwell family moves to Ohio in May; Elizabeth's father dies on August 6.

1845 Elizabeth's friend and neighbor encourages her to pursue a career in medicine.

1847 Elizabeth is admitted to Geneva Medical College in New York.

1848 Elizabeth works at Blockley Almshouse, a hospital for poor people in Philadelphia, Pennsylvania.

1849 Elizabeth becomes the first woman in the United States to earn a medical degree on January 23; she enters La Maternité in Paris, France. She contracts a serious eye infection.

1850 Elizabeth goes to a hydrotherapy clinic in June to recuperate from her eye infection. After two months, the eye becomes inflamed and has to be removed. Elizabeth is fitted with a glass eye. In October, she resumes her studies, this time at St. Bartholomew's Hospital in London.

1851 Elizabeth meets and befriends Florence Nightingale. In July, she returns to New York and opens a medical practice.

1854 Elizabeth adopts her daughter, Kitty; she opens the New York Dispensary for Poor Women and Children.

1857 Elizabeth founds the New York Infirmary for Women and Children with her sister Dr. Emily Blackwell.

1861 The Civil War begins; Elizabeth helps organize the U.S. Sanitary Aid Commission (with Dorothea Dix).

1865 The Civil War ends.

1868 Elizabeth founds the New York Infirmary Women's Medical College.

1869 Elizabeth moves to Europe, where she remains most of the rest of her life.

1876 The American Medical Association accepts its first female member, Sarah Hackett Stevenson.

1895 Elizabeth's autobiography, *Pioneer Work in Opening the Medical Profession to Women,* is published.

1905 Only 4 percent of medical school graduates are women.

1910 Elizabeth dies in Hastings, England, on May 31.

1943 Gerty Cori, M.D. is the first woman to win the Nobel Prize in Medicine.

1989 The American Medical Association opens a Women in Medicine Office.

1990 Antonia Novello, M.D., becomes the first woman to be appointed the U.S. Surgeon General.

1998 Dr. Nancy Dickey becomes the first female president of the American Medical Association.

2003 Nearly half the applicants for medical school are women.

2006 Women make up 27.8 percent of all doctors in the United States.

2008 The United Kingdom has more females than males in medical schools. Male doctors urge schools to begin recruiting more male students.

A CONVERSATION WITH
Julie Gerberding

In July 2002, Dr. Julie Gerberding was appointed the first female director of the Centers for Disease Control and Prevention (CDC)—the federal agency responsible for protecting the nation's health. Here, Dr. Gerberding talks about Elizabeth Blackwell's legacy.

Q. What made you decide to become a doctor?

A. I have a very soft heart, and when I was very young I was always so sad when someone I cared about was ill. I also took in every wounded animal I found—birds with broken wings, orphaned baby rabbits, and forlorn puppies. My grandmother taught me to love all of nature, and with that came a strong interest in the natural sciences that my parents encouraged. These characteristics all came together when I was about 4 years old, and that's when I knew I wanted to be a doctor.

Q. When did you first learn about Elizabeth Blackwell and her role as the first woman doctor in America?

A. I first learned about Elizabeth Blackwell when I studied some of the work that Florence Nightingale accomplished. Dr. Blackwell and Ms. Nightingale were friends and shared a passion for doing everything they could to help patients.

Q. How significant was Elizabeth Blackwell's achievement and how did she change the future for women in medicine?

A. Someone always has to go first—to pave the way for the others that come behind them. Dr. Blackwell paved the way for the first generation of woman physicians in America.

Q. How has the role of women in medicine changed in the past 150 years?

A. Today women in medicine have unlimited opportunities—there is virtually no path that can't be taken. But there still are some realities—women in medicine are not as likely to have the top jobs, or to reach the highest levels in schools of medicine. One reason for this is that women who are raising children are not promoted at the same rate as men.

Q. What challenges do you think Elizabeth Blackwell faced that women do not face today?

A. She had to overcome many misunderstandings about the roles that women can have in society that women today are less likely to face. In Dr. Blackwell's time, it was very unusual for women to have a professional career. Today that is not an issue for most women in America, though it is an issue in many other parts of the world.

Q. What obstacles did you have to overcome to achieve your goals and how did you overcome them?

A. I was lucky to have a very supportive family, wonderful teachers in my small-town school, and superb faculty at Case Western Reserve University (CWRU) to mentor me along the way. Probably a big hurdle was financial—but I was able to attend a private school thanks to generous family members and CWRU alumni.

Q. As the first woman to become director of the Centers for Disease Control, you are also a pioneer. What are your immediate goals and what would you like your legacy to be?

A. Three words: commit—to excellence in everything you do; connect—with people outside your core team to create a whole greater than the sum of the parts; and care—passionately and deeply about the people you serve.

Q. Why should we read about Elizabeth Blackwell today?

A. History informs us, provides perspective, and teaches important, timeless lessons.

Q. What aspect of Elizabeth Blackwell's personality do you think helped her succeed? Why?

A. She was obviously courageous, tenacious, dedicated to a cause, and never, never gave up.

GLOSSARY

abolitionist: a person who works to end slavery

anatomy: the study of the human body

antibiotic: an agent, usually medicine, that destroys bacteria

antiseptic: an agent used to control bacteria, such as washing to reduce the chance of infection

apprentice: a trainee or learner in a skill or trade

cholera: a disease that attacks the intestines

commencement: a graduation ceremony

depression: an economic slump

diagnose: to identify a specific disease or condition in a patient

epidemic: a fast-spreading disease

governess: someone who takes care of another person's child or children

infection: the state of disease or a condition caused by bacteria in the body

infirmary: a hospital or clinic

internship: the chance for advanced students to learn about their field in the appropriate setting, as with a doctor during an internship at a hospital

literary: relating to literature or reading

malaria: a disease with fever and chills that is carried by mosquitoes

midwife: a person whose occupation is delivering babies

obstetrician: a doctor whose main business is caring for pregnant women and delivering their babies

pioneer: a person who is among the first to explore or enter into a new area of activity

refinery: a factory for processing raw materials, such as sugar or petroleum

reformer: someone who works for change

suffragist: a person who works to gain the right to vote for women

thesis: a long academic paper or essay

typhus: a disease that features high fevers, coughing, headaches, and other symptoms

vaccination: the process of giving a person or an animal immunity from a specific disease

valedictory: a farewell speech often given at graduations

vivisection: the practice of performing operations on live animals for the purpose of medical or scientific research

FOR MORE INFORMATION

BOOKS AND OTHER RESOURCES

Abram, Ruth. *Send Us a Lady Physician: Women Doctors in America, 1835–1920.* New York: W. W. Norton & Company, Inc., 1985.

Binns, Tristan Boyer. *Elizabeth Blackwell: First Woman Physician.* Danbury, Connecticut: Franklin Watts Library, 2005.

Blackwell, Elizabeth. *Pioneer Work in Opening the Medical Profession to Women.* Amherst, New York: Humanity Books, 2005.

Glimm, Adele. *Elizabeth Blackwell: First Woman Doctor of Modern Times.* Columbus, Ohio: McGraw-Hill, 2000.

Kent, Deborah, and Eric v. d. Luft. *Elizabeth Blackwell: Physician and Health Educator.* Chanhassen, Minnesota: Child's World, 2003.

Robbins, Trina. *Elizabeth Blackwell: America's First Woman Doctor.* Mankato, Minnesota: Capstone Press, 2007.

WEB SITES

Hobart & William Smith Colleges
campus.hws.edu/his/blackwell/biography.html
Visit this site to learn more about Elizabeth's work in medicine.

The National Library of Medicine
www.nlm.nih.gov/hmd/blackwell/index.htm
This site includes biographical data about Elizabeth's early classroom experiences and is presented like a museum tour.

SELECT BIBLIOGRAPHY AND SOURCE NOTES

Abram, Ruth. *Send Us a Lady Physician: Women Doctors in America, 1835–1920.* N.Y.: W. W. Norton & Company, Inc., 1985.

Binns, Tristan Boyer. *Elizabeth Blackwell: First Woman Physician.* Danbury, Conn.: Franklin Watts Library, 2005.

Blackwell, Elizabeth. *Pioneer Work in Opening the Medical Profession to Women.* Amherst, N.Y.: Humanity Books, 2005.

Glimm, Adele. *Elizabeth Blackwell: First Woman Doctor of Modern Times.* Columbus, Ohio: McGraw-Hill, 2000.

Kent, Deborah, and Eric v. d. Luft. *Elizabeth Blackwell: Physician and Health Educator.* Chanhassen, Minn.: Child's World, 2003.

LeClair, Mary K., Justin D. White, and Susan Keeter. *Three 19th Century Women Doctors.* Syracuse, N.Y.: Hofmann Press, 2007.

Robbins, Trina. *Elizabeth Blackwell: America's First Woman Doctor.* Mankato, Minn.: Capstone Press, 2007.

PAGE 2

http://womenshistory.about.com/od/quotes/a/eliz_blackwell.htm

CHAPTER ONE

Page 8, line 1: Henry Blackwell, letter, January 23, 1849, as quoted in Blackwell, Elizabeth. *Pioneer Work in Opening the Medical Profession to Women.* Amherst, N.Y.: Humanity Books, 2005, p. 129

Page 8, line 21: Delancy, Margaret Munro, letter, January 28, 1849, as quoted in "Dr. Elizabeth Blackwell's Graduation—An Eye-Witness Account," accessed at http://campus.hws.edu/his/blackwell/history/graduation.html, p. 3

Page 9, line 14: Blackwell. *Pioneer Work*, p. 130

Page 9, line 21: DeLancey. "Dr. Elizabeth Blackwell's Graduation—An Eye-Witness Account," p. 3

Page 9, line 24: Lee, Charles A. "Valedictory Address to the Graduating Class, Geneva Medical College," January 23, 1849, p. 28

Page 11, line 13: D.K., "The Late Medical Degree to a Female," *Boston Medical and Surgical Journal*, accessed at www.nlm.nih.gov/hmd/blackwell/Anti.jpg

Page 11, line 20: "An M.D. in a Gown," *Punch*, 1849, accessed at www.nlm.nih.gov/hmd/blackwell

CHAPTER TWO

Page 17, line 20: Boyd, Julia. *The Excellent Doctor Blackwell: The Life of the First Woman Physician.* Gloucestershire, England: Sutton Publishing Ltd., 2005, p. 6

Page 20, line 8: Blackwell. *Pioneer Work*, p. 58

Page 21, sidebar: "Judgment Day," part 4, *Africans in America*, www.pbs.org/wgbh/aia/part4/4p1561.html

Page 23, line 13: Boyd. p. 24

Page 23, line 18: Ibid., p. 26

Page 25, line 10: Ibid., pp. 31-32

Page 27, line 3: Blackwell. *Pioneer Work*, pp. 64–65

Page 27, line 16: Ibid., p. 68

Page 28, line 10: Ibid., p. 74

Page 29, line 7: Blackwell. *Pioneer Work*, p. 74

Page 29, sidebar: "Harriett Beecher Stowe's Life & Time," Harriett Beecher Stowe Center, www.harrietbeecherstowecenter.org/life/#uncle

Page 30, line 7: Blackwell. *Pioneer Work*, p. 29

Page 31, line 6: Ibid., p. 88

Page 31, line 21: Ibid., p. 75

CHAPTER FOUR

Page 36, line 6: Blackwell. *Pioneer Work*, p. 66

Page 37, line 7: Stephen Smith, M.D., "The Medical Co-Education of the Sexes," *Church Union*, as quoted in Blackwell, *Pioneer Work*, p. 279

Page 37, line 20: Blackwell. *Pioneer Work*, pp. 110, 111

Page 38, line 12: Ibid., p. 113

Page 40, line 1: Blackwell. *Pioneer Work*, p. 70

Page 40, line 9: Ibid., p. 69

Page 41, line 2: Ibid., p. 80

CHAPTER FIVE

Page 45, line 6: Blackwell, *Pioneer Work*, p. 136

Page 46, line 7: Ibid., p. 151

Page 47, line 4: Boyd. *The Excellent Doctor Blackwell: The Life of the First Woman Physician*, p. 104

Page 48, line 21: Blackwell, *Pioneer Work*, p. 176

Page 49, line 14: Ibid., pp. 187–188

Page 52, line 12: Ibid., p. 170

Page 52, line 18: Ibid., p. 172

Page 53, line 4: Blackwell. *Pioneer Work*, p. 200

Page 54, line 3: Ibid., p. 172

Page 57, line 4: Ibid., p. 176

CHAPTER SIX

Page 59, line 13: Blackwell. *Pioneer Work*, p. 223

Page 60, line 21: Ibid., p. 226

Page 66, line 9: Boyd. *The Excellent Doctor Blackwell: The Life of the First Woman Physician*, p. 137

Page 67, line 8: Ibid., p. 170

Page 68, line 3: Ibid., p. 175

CHAPTER SEVEN

Page 76, line 4: Boyd. *The Excellent Doctor Blackwell: The Life of the First Woman Physician*, p. 187

Page 77, line 5: Ibid., pp. 193–194

Page 79, line 17: Ibid., p. 191

CHAPTER EIGHT

Page 84, line 4: Blackwell, Elizabeth. Letter to Barbara Bodichon, October 4, 1874, Columbia University Library

Page 85, line 23: Blackwell, Elizabeth. *Essays in Medical Sociology*. N.Y.: Arno Press, 1972, p. 146

Page 86, line 6: Ibid., p. 207

Page 89, line 18: Blackwell. *Pioneer Work*, p. 32

CHAPTER NINE

Page 93, line 15: "Elizabeth Blackwell Obituary." *London Times*, June 1, 1910

Page 96, sidebar: "NY Downtown Hospital Restructures with Lessons Learned on 9/11," http://www.downtownhospital.org/pages/3142/NY1_News:_NY_Downtown_Hospital_Restructures_With_Lessons_Learned_On_9/11_-_8/28/06.htm

Page 97, line 20: Blackwell, Elizabeth. "Inspiring Quotes by Women," www.feminist.com/resources/quotes/

INDEX

ABOUT THE AUTHOR

Barbara A. Somervill writes a full range of nonfiction materials—from biographies to nature books, from video scripts to educational texts. She loves writing about people because she finds out the most interesting things about their lives. When not working on a writing project, Ms. Somervill is an avid duplicate bridge player, reader, and moviegoer.

She lived in New York, Canada, Australia, and California before settling in the foothills of the Blue Ridge Mountains with her husband and her dog, Sydney.

PICTURE CREDITS